WE SAY WE LOVE EACH OTHER

Other books by the author:

Rebellion, Essays 1980-1991
Crime Against Nature
Yours In Struggle (co-author)

WE SAY WE LOVE EACH OTHER

Poetry by

MINNIE BRUCE PRATT

Firebrand Books
Ithaca, New York

Some of these poems, in slightly different versions, have previously appeared in *Feminary, IKON,* and *Sinister Wisdom.*

Originally published by Spinsters/*Aunt Lute,* this edition (1992) is published by Firebrand Books.

Book design by Pam Wilson Design Studio
Cover design by Lee Tackett
Typesetting by ComText Typography and Bets Ltd.

Printed in the United States on acid-free paper by McNaughton & Gunn

Library of Congress Cataloging-in-Publication Data

Pratt, Minnie Bruce.
We say we love each other / Minnie Bruce Pratt.
p. cm.
ISBN 1-56341-024-9. — ISBN 1-56341-023-0 (pbk.)
1. Lesbians—Poetry. I. Title.
[PS3566.R35W4 1992]
811'.54—dc 92-24947
CIP

ACKNOWLEDGMENTS

I would like to thank Joan E. Biren, Elly Bulkin, Judith McDaniel, and the many women who talked to me after poetry readings, for their conversations with me about this work. Grateful thanks also to Jean Swallow for her editorial guidance, to Nanette Gartrell and Dee Mosbacher for their friendship, and to Nancy K. Bereano for her continued confidence in and support for my work.

This book is for Joan—*was, is, will be.*

CONTENTS

READING MAPS: ONE

for Elly

Yesterday Nettie in my office talked about summer
school, her geography course, how before she hadn't
really known where she was, whether she went
east or south to get to the beach, didn't know
how to read a map, Ezra always did that.
She said, *I never had any need to read*
a map, every place I go it's already charted.

I drive to work down the boulevard. The way
does not lead through trees, no dark crossed limbs
sprouting green flesh. Over my head
a grey net hangs, suspended, lines
from Duke Power wired from pole to pole.
I have learned what to expect at every turn.
The morning headlines again have read *WOMAN*
KILLED: wild chase across town, her car
forced off the road by a truck, her husband,
a sergeant from the army base, with a rifle. She ran
into the woods. He followed and shot her in the head,
walked back to his pickup, drove away.

I want to drive away from this town. At my back
to the north men fall from the sky. Parachutes
burst open like nylon morning glories.
In the webbing men jerk at lines to float
closer to their targets. *If I had an M-16*
I could go shoot them down.

To my left
the Putt-Putt course is open. On zig-zags
of green indoor-outdoor carpet, young men
demonstrate their skill to girlfriends: how to hit
a small ball into a hole curbed by painted brick.

I think of my lovers who have been raped. *I could*
castrate each man there.

On my right, women
shop at the Winn-Dixie between walls of stacked cans.
G.I. wives stand in the cash register line
with ladies from Lakeshore Drive who will not speak.
If I drove the car through the window they would
speak, open mouths, stare at nothing
left of the plate glass but a corner of webbed cracks.

Two miles ahead, at the corner where the boulevard runs
into Hay Street, is a church, empty now. *With spare gas*
in a jug, rags, I could roll a ball of fire
under the porch. Tomorrow there might be no pulpit,
no door for women to enter, to turn down the aisle
toward narrow pew.

But at that corner other women
still walk for a living, down where I have sat stopped
at a red light, seen a woman step to the double
yellow line, straighten the black seam of a stocking,
pull her skirt, purple silk parachute, up
over her head. *I thought she hid in her hand*
a grenade, ready to blow up the man and herself.
Then the light changed; the street looked the same.

I will not drive downtown today. I am afraid
there has been no change, that my anger and despair
may ignite like a mass of oiled rags. *I might*
walk into an intersection and burst into flames.

I turn left after A & H Cleaners,
rebuilt from the bombing five years back,
first business owned by a Black man on the avenue.
Behind the red sign, gold letters, promises
of one-hour service, Black women press
knife-sharp creases into army fatigues.
White men I despise already have been here with fire.
I see their image in my rear-view mirror,
see my own burning, the will to violence.

I want us all to change; yet I drive to work
the same way every morning, doors locked,
windows rolled up, afraid. *I want to roll my anger*
like a tank over terrain I do not control.
I forget that I have resisted, that I have imagined
how to travel a different way.

                                        I turn left
at Filter Plant Road, past the telephone pole
with kudzu snaking green up its guy wires.

When I get to work, the papers on my desk lie
ruled by thin blue lines, scrawled over
with tendrils of pencil and ink: *I had to get this job*
to leave my husband. For weeks I could not think
what to put in the white spaces on the application blank,
years of never knowing where I was,
years of marriage when he drove and I tried
to read the map, to see my body in relation
to the space around me, to find it on the diagram:
green boundaries for grassland, forest, parks,
yellow for cities, red for Indian reservation
or military base, red lines for scenic routes,
grey for time zones. *I had no belief*
that I could get myself from here to there.
I would say left for right until at some inter-
section in Colorado or Georgia he would reach
over and take the map. I did not try
to take it back. I did not know I was angry

until I began to talk to other women, get directions
from them on how to meet. They called me: voices travelled
over the phone, spiralled into the labyrinth, my inner ear
that sat like a snail, listening. They repeated
turns and streets. I wrote their words down,
then propped the sheet of paper on the seat beside me
as I drove,

            once for hours on Bragg Boulevard
to find Johnson Road by the cleaners in Bonnie Doone.

At a red light I stopped short of a carload of men:
paratroopers out on the town could slash lines
finer than wrinkles on a woman's face, or fasten
her genitals with copper wire to their battery. *I had*
to locate women friends.

I began to guess
at turns. Landmarks blurred, perhaps remembered
by my guide in a different pattern, perhaps not clearly seen
by me in the rain, yellow light from massage parlors
streaking the windshield. I slowed down to read
my map under moving streetlights. I was determined
to find the house where women met to tell
our secrets, pieces of life torn out, hidden,
or almost thrown away. *If I could find them,*
they might show me the way out.

That night
I refused to be lost and got to Denise's apartment.
The words on my scrap of paper matched the address
on the door: *Grand Prix Drive, 2105-C.*
Inside six women sat in a maze of chrome and plexiglass.
They looked like me; I didn't trust them.
As we talked, the windows rattled: not thunder but artillery.
The woman across from me looked directly at me;
blue shadows painted around her eyes did not hide
her glance; her jaw tensed under its camouflage of rouge.
She opened her mouth and began to speak.

The room shifted around me to other places
as we hunted our fragments scattered on the scorched earth,
men's land, as we gathered the bones of memory:
how her mother forgot the five years before electroshock,
how she moved out and her boyfriend burned
her clothes and books in the front yard, how the rapist
held a lighter to her hair, how my husband chopped
up the kitchen chairs with an axe and burned them.
I saw the ashes in the back yard when I got home,
what was left of three red chairs; I was glad
it wasn't the remains of me and the children.

In the narrow kitchen I told him I did not want
the place he gave me in the world as it was.
He spoke of change, of going from here to there
with me. *I did not want to leave him behind;*
I did not want to be in the same room when he spoke
with the mouth I had loved for nine years, with the voice
I had hated when it cracked like bones breaking from anger.
He was the same man who shared two small boys, the laundry,
dishes, the man who smashed a bowl on the counter
beside me, left a fist of blue fragments on red tile,
the man who leaned with me against the yellow wall
and cried, his tears streaking my cheek, the same man,
in a three-piece suit, who asked, smiling,
about the revolution while I fixed a mimeograph machine
on the kitchen table.

I wanted to slash his face
with the bread knife. I did not raise my voice.
My hand kept on turning the crank. Sheets
of cheap paper stared up from the floor, lines
slightly blurred, stubborn, black as charcoal:
"Marriage Equality Act 1976,"
"Joanne Little Acquitted," "New book:
Mama Doesn't Live Here Any More," "Lesbian
film: Jan Oxenberg's Home Movie."

When I finally yelled and he shoved me against the stove,
out the door, it was like any of our drives together,
like sex: one minute I was in my own body, the next,
outside myself, displaced, while he took control.
After I hit the floor of the back porch, I saw
my family at the far end of the kitchen, looking
at me as if I were at the wrong end of a telescope,
he rigid as a granite marker at a boundary,
the children crying, flesh of my flesh, their faces
not yet hardened, looking at me flat on my back
in the geography of power. I felt the grab of his hands on
my arm, the hands that had rubbed my aching back.

The porch cement was cool under my bleeding arm;
I thought I might just lie there on the quiet slab.
I could smell the back yard, the dusty smell

of sasanquas, the rotting leaves gone to earth,
smell of the memory: all living things
change themselves. *He could be different,*
but he wasn't. I would be.
I got to my feet. Behind me the back steps
led into the night, into terror and unknown ventures.

I moved out when, fingers sweated around
a ball-point pen, I made myself real
enough on paper to get this job and leave him.
Now I live alone just off the boulevard.
Early in the morning I watch the shadow of pine
needles brush fine lines over my bedroom wall.
I wonder about my charred and smoking heart:
what grows in a burned-over forest. Sometimes I sleep
with a lover, my bed an island in the water of night.
With my hand between her breasts, near her heart,
I dream of a place green, flourishing, where we
live safe. At meetings I look for women
who look at me. Our glances catch, like the wind
and seeds poised in the open milkweed pod.

Tonight as I leave work, as streetlights arc
pink over the boulevard, I hardly remember the dream.
The evening headlines read *WOMAN'S CHARRED*
BODY SHOVED INSIDE INCINERATOR. I pass a white woman
driving a Continental, a Black woman in the backseat.
I meet my neighbor Sheila on her way to third shift.
To feed herself and three children she delivers
pizza, passes between barracks lined up like tanks,
balances herself between rows of soldiers saying
Baby come on and *Don't talk that way to a lady.*
She's never liked the way the place is laid out
but she knows how to get around. *But I want to go*

outside this landscape, drive right off the map.
I don't know the next turn. The street
looks the same as any other day I wanted to change it,
on my right, the cement block building marked
topless, stenciled with naked women. A man
in khaki enters; in ten years, he may turn

and show me the face of one of my sons.
And what will I do then? What then, what now?

I can only resist the need to destroy
that spreads anger and despair heavy as asphalt
through my veins, makes me a road driven over by violence,
makes me a map of someone else's world.
I will remember that I have learned to travel
a different way.

Five years ago I was afraid
to cross town; tonight I drive down the boulevard
to a room where snakeplants grow from the wall,
where I eat green-fleshed avocado, and I talk
to women who sketch quick lines over the paper
ridges of a napkin. Our faces have begun to wrinkle,
our eyes are webbed in lines. We trace the anger
flying through our bodies back to its point of origin.
We locate forbidden places, the kind marked *dangerous*
swamp, unknown territory on the old charts.
We plot change. We love one another.
Our bodies become lodestones to the future. *We imagine*
a place not marked yet on any map. Between us
words tremble and veer, like the iron needle
of a compass, a guide to what we are making real.

1981

SHARING THE EYE

for D.M. and L.N.

I

We live between the county speedway and the interstate
in a brick house with azaleas that foam
orange and pink under our windows in the spring;
the roses we mulch with pine straw in the summer.
A repairman who came thought we were sisters,
three daughters of a man he knew on Churchill Drive.
When we go out in the evening to walk around the block,
we look quite ordinary, young women in tennis shoes,
no bared teeth, no glaring eyes or protruding tongues.
But the neighbors think it's odd that we live alone.
They mean: without men. They think we're three weird women.

We walk until the weather changes. The purple blazing star
turns brown, the wind begins to rise. Then we come inside.
We sit apart from each other but not separate. We hear
the wind rush over our heads through the tops of the pines,
like the tide coming in: constant, inconstant waves, the ocean
rising and running a long way inland. The pines bend.
They twist, seaweed in the wind, stands of kelp in the waves.

Inside the wind, we talk or we don't. We take thought
from each other. We write our lives over in flimsy notebooks.
The lamp holds us in a round glance of light, the pages
yellow as quartz, our words written as if on unpolished stone.

II

Once there were three women who lived together
on a small island of rock above the aurora borealis
where waves of purple, red and orange light
splashed against them with the constant sea spray
glazing their dark skin until they toughened

to glitter with the iridescent chitin of dragonflies.
Their hair coiled and hissed and crept
in the wind that always blew around them.

These women saw whatever they looked at,
knew it as entirely as any granite pebble
that they picked up on their beach, passed
from hand to hand, considered and put aside.
They were cunning, wide-roaming, strong.
They had the power to see between truth and lie.

Some terrified men began the rumor
their looks could kill, their unmasked faces were
ugly enough to turn men to stone,
their hair was undulant, unbound, monstrous.

The young man who set out to kill one
got directions from three grey women
with a single eye between them. The eye was sharp,
could see through stones and men, but the women
quarreled as they passed it from hand to hand
and the boy stole it until they told him the way.

He got his tools from three young women.
Flattered by his interest, with gleaming eyes
they gave him the power of invisible flight
and a woven, embroidered pouch
that could expand to hold a woman's head.

At the island he caught the three women asleep,
the wind and their hair sliding against the rock.
He killed one, cut her head off, stuffed it in his bag.
When he wanted to command complete attention,
he held her up, dangling, in his hand.

The power dimmed but did not fail from her sight.

III

At midnight the pines are unmoving in the air,
cold stillness around them as water in the ocean deeps.

In our house I wake up, yelling in my throat,
a woman by my bed, another at the door.

I tell them it's the same old fear: myself asleep,
the man with a knife shoving in the screen door,
my mouth open but no sound, my eyelids stretched wide,
my look useless, unable to stop what I see.

One woman says: *We heard you and we came.*
The other tells her dream:

She balances on a rocky slope at the crest of a hill,
sliding but staying up, above everything,
the wind blazing over her naked skin.

Men huddle at the bottom, discuss how to reach her,
but at the attempt each slips and falls
down the glittering side.

She balances on the crest of a shining hill,
at the top of a glassy, falling but never falling, wave.
She laughs. She has never felt so strong.

For awhile the three of us sit quietly on my bed.
The thought comes to me with the click of a thrown pebble
heard in darkness: we can yet dream and wake and act.

IV

Toward morning the sky is black as the abyss
where the squid swims, tentacles and arms twisting,
where she turns the water around her to luminous cloud
like the grey that soon will spread from the east.

Just before this hour a woman cries out and I wake,
to hear no intruder but a passionate motion: the other women
behind the closed door of their room. In terror I hear
them tangle together with twisting mouths. Open,
opening in the eye of orgasm, closed. They are finding out
truth or the lie. In terror I remember the weapon of sex,
my body worn as a grotesque mask, the clumsy betrayal,
and then sleep.

The room is entirely dark, and smells of roses,
dried roses in the brass bowl. Tell the truth,
terror has not been all: there is the longed-for gulf,
skin writhing down to stone, eye of the vagina staring,
a woman's sharpened ecstatic face, a look like my own.

I lie awake in the silence. Far above, the stars toss
in brilliance, the phosphorescence of gulfstream currents.
I finger my tiny clitoral pebble and drift to an edge:
spiral of nebulae, funnel of water, collapsing walls
when spirit and matter go hissing together through the house.

In the north above the pines, a star dims and brightens,
unmasked in the cold morning, ancient repetitive guardian eye.

V

Morning light drips down the spiny needles of the pines.

I get up early. Light from the nearest sun slants
in the kitchen window. Through the curtains the yellow
changes to stark green of coiled leaves, indigo, red, orange.

I will soon leave the other women, now wrapped in sleep.
We will live separate and seldom visit except to tell
stories. What powers have they taught me?

I bend to my cup's mirror of tea. Steam tumbles up
in hot grey curls. But in the oily surface
my reflected, distorted eyes and mouth are dumb.

The water boils, hissing. The grey cat watches
me make soup. I peel off an onion's silk skin.
In my hands its heavy roundness is a lump of milky quartz,

polished, opaque, too thick to look into for the future.
Divided, its layers are translucent water if held to the sun.
A green spark of what might happen is at the center.

1980

WAULKING SONG: ONE

Waulking tunes are sung by groups of Hebridean women as they work woolen cloth with their hands and feet to strengthen its weave. The women measure their task by the number of songs needed to complete the work, rather than by minutes or hours. Each waulking song has a narrative which may be altered by the lead singer, as well as a unique refrain so ancient that the meanings of its syllables have been lost; the refrains below may have been sung by women at work as much as a thousand years ago.

Maighread Ni Lachainn, I found you buried
face down, as I looked for those like myself.

Twelve motherings past, men placed you
face down in the dirt, a witch and a poet.

They said there was not much left
of you or your songs, your vehement spirit.

Hao ri o hù ò,
Ro ho i o hì ò.

Down the black coast of Skye you made your way
with tossing words that measured work

for women who waulked, querned, or spun,
each task measured with lengths of song.

With you travelled another woman
who set your words to the slap of a tune.

In summer you lay at night in the shieling,
her blue brooch unclasped, your plaid on the rushes;

the mud-draggled ends put from her,
your knees almost fractured from the day's walking.

O ho i o hì ò,
Hao ri o hù ò.

In winter you sheltered with spotted goats,
between their bed and yours a curtain of wattle,

their breath your warmth, their rank milk your food.
You waited alone in the peat's blue smoke.

At the proper moment the poem came.
You saw each word run along the green turf

where roof joined stone wall. You saw the spell
that each word worked in the body's chamber.

Hao ri o hù ò,
Ro ho i o hì ò,

When storms sped faster than gulls on the coast,
the women came for word of the ships.

You went to the cave at the Sound of the Ulva.
With clenched eyes, you sent your spirit to search.

You saw past the others, you spoke the unwanted:
men's bodies beaten to thin seaweed on the cliffs.

Some said you were mad, that a shift in the wind
had blown out your soul, candle in the cave.

Strong-willed, *aigeannach*, you gave them the word
like a pinch of your snuff, your fingers stained brown.

O ho i o hì ò,
Hao ri o hù ò.

They beat urine-soaked cloth to tighten its weave.
They kept time with your songs, even after your death.

Hao ri o hù ò,
Ro ho i o hì ò.

1980

WAULKING SONG: TWO

for C.S.

I

É hó hì ura bhì,
Ho ro ho ì, o ho ro ho.

At first she would not answer
when I asked what was wrong.

Then she told what had happened
that afternoon when she went in to work.

Ho ro ho ì, ó ho ro ho,
É hó hì ura bhì.

Later she gave me the shirt to mend,
a thin K-Mart cotton

with lines of yellow blue and red
running from grey to brighter plaid.

É hó hì ura bhì,
Ho ro ho ì, o ho ro ho.

She had worn it the winter we met.
Under the lines I felt her heart beat.

Many times I had held her and felt
her heart beating beneath that thin cloth.

Ho ro ho ì, ó ho ro ho,
É hó hì ura bhì.

II

Ì u ru rù bhi u o,
Hó í abh o.

In the summer haze she had gone to work.
The man with the knife stopped her.

He shoved her from the door to the straggling hedge.
He jerked at her shirt and ripped the seams.

Chalain éileadh ò hi o,
Ro ho leathag.

He cut the buttons off one by one.
He raped her and tried to cut her throat.

He tried to cut her throat. And he did.
The red of her blood crossed the plaid of her shirt.

Ì u ru rù bhi u o,
Hó í abh o.

He asked if she liked it.
When she would not say yes,

he glinted the knife and he laughed.
He laughed and he left. She lay in the dust,

smoked a cigarette, got up,
went home to her trailer, took a bath.

She washed the shirt, put it away,
and looked to see what else was torn.

Chalain éileadh ò hi o,
Ro ho leathag.

III

O ho i o hì ò,
Hao ri o hù ò.

We swore his knife would not part us,
yet fear divided us with many blades.

She did not want me to touch her,
to feel semen and dirt on her skin.

When I moved suddenly, she saw
the sun flash on the knife blade.

She wanted to know where
my hands were at all times.

When I slept with my arm around her,
she dreamed he had her pinned down

and woke night after night saying *no*,
night after night saying *no*.

She feared that I would not touch her,
would not touch, and that I would.

Hao ri o hù ò,
Ro ho i o hì ò.

I wanted the red mark to peel
off her throat like a band-aid

so she would be her self
without this pain: unscarred, unchanged,

not a woman who could have been
dead behind a QuickStop store

a line of ants running from her neck,
a woman her friends would not touch.

Ro ho i o hì ò,
O ho i o hì ò.

After three months we wanted her
over it, to be done with dying

while she heard her rape each time
a rock cracked under feet behind her

as she crossed an empty parking lot.
I heard her death each time

a friend spoke the word *rape*
as matter-of-fact as the evening news.

O ho i o hì ò,
Hao ri o hù ò.

That winter, on weekends, when we shared a bed,
we shared bad dreams. We twisted in sheets.

Some nights she heard her voice cry out
and woke herself, breath tearing her throat.

Some nights I felt her shake beside me,
caught in the hedge in December wind.

Before I touched her, I called her name
to wake her before his hand could reach.

We held hands as we talked in the dark.
The shirt lay folded, unmended, in my drawer.

Hao ri o hù ò,
Ro ho i o hì ò.

IV

O ho ì ù ó,
Air fair all ill ó ho.

It has been three years; the shirt
was mended, not thrown away.

We rise at dawn to dress for work.
I touch her bare arm. She is alive.

Her heartbeats rush under my fingers.
Her flesh is solid, not crumbled to dust.

Air fair all ill ó ho,
Ro ho hao ri rì ó.

Under my hands, her shoulders spread,
broad, an outcrop of limestone,

under her skin, layers of muscle,
from heft and lift, the weight of her work.

She has made herself strong, enough
to knock a man down, enough

to tell me one night what his hands
had done, the exact, secret wounds.

Ro ho hao ri rì ó,
O ho ì ù ó.

I wanted my hands to be rain for her
to wash away all hurt, the trace of blood.

I did what I could. I took out the shirt,
sewed the buttons back on, one by one,

sewed over each seam, twice, by hand.
He would not ruin what we had made.

O ho ì ú ó,
Air fair all ill ó ho.

She wore the shirt, walked alone to her job.
She would not live in tatters and shreds.

But some afternoons he got his death:
when we heard of a nurse off work, the men,

blackberry vines in an empty lot;
a woman raped at the Gulf station,

stabbed through both eyes with a screwdriver
so she would not see to find him later.

Air fair all ill ó ho,
Ro ho hao ri rì ó.

Then we could not bear witness to our life.
We bought beer and drank to become like stone,

no live woman or dead in our touch.
We cried out with the voice of falling rocks.

We fell asleep, dead weight, in each other's arms,
but always we swore that we would wake up.

Ro ho hao ri rì ó,
O ho ì ù ó.

It has been three years: I wake before dawn
in the dark. I think of the mended shirt.

It still hangs in her closet, the pattern
of red blue yellow lines seamed together.

Her scar has faded to a thin white line.
I can touch her breast. I can feel her heart beating.

He has not ruined what we have made.
At dawn we will rise to dress for work.

O ho ì ù ó,
Air fair all ill ó ho.

V

Hao ri o hù ò,
Ro ho i o hì ò.

When she got to work at five til 8
this morning, a woman named Millie was shot

in the parking lot as she left her car.
The man with the gun watched her blood

disappear into the asphalt. Her boss,
other women watched from a doorway.

At first she asked for help. The man
left to rape a woman in the next street.

In emergency she fought with nurses
who held her to the cart, said *Lie down*.

She said *I know I'm dying. I want*
to sit up. And she did, before she died,

while they were saying *Be quiet, you'll be better.*
She was a secretary, three months pregnant.

Ro ho i o hì ò,
O ho i o hì ò.

Do you want me to be quiet? You are tired
of the words *blood, rape, death*.

So am I. I had ended these lines
at the last refrain, but this morning I heard

about Millie. I remembered again your blood
in the dirt, your stomach exposed to the knife.

I want to keep harm from you. I want
to clothe and protect you with my arms.

I look at my hands that held needle and thread.
We resist by whatever means we can.

At work your arm has thrust, your hand
has hefted two feet of steel pipe

over a counter at the man who threatened.
You say *Next time I fight back even if I die.*

Your hands are not quiet; your voice is angry.
I love you because you have refused to die.

O ho i o hì ò,
Hao ri o hù ò.

This poem is for you, to pin to the mended shirt,
like the paper slip you find in a new pocket,

#49, but you know it's a woman,
all day folding sleeves around cardboard.

At work almost dead on her feet,
she folds the plaid thin fabrics.

She thinks of what her hands make at home.
When she leaves the line, the machines are silent.

Her steps make a poem to the rhythm of her heart,
like a poem for you, to pin to the mended shirt.

Hao ri o hù ò,
Ro ho i o hì ò.

1982

SHARP GLASS

for M. B.

Shattered glass in the street at Maryland and 10th:
smashed sand glittering on a beach of black asphalt.

You can think of it so: or as bits of broken kaleidoscope,
or as crystals spilled from the white throat of a geode.

You can use metaphor to move the glass as far as possible
from the raised hands that threw the bottle

for their own reasons of amusement, or despair, or the desire
to make a cymbal crash in the ears of midnight sleepers.

Or you can use words like your needle, the probe curious
in tough heels, your bare feet having walked in risky places.

You can work to the surface the irritant, pain, the glass
sliver to blink in the light, sharp as a question.

1983

I DO NOT WAIT

for I. Y.

I don't expect I'll ever see you naked
although you tell me half-secrets about your body,
fear for your left breast, scars or early death.
Your clothed outline is vivid, face and hands black
against purple velvet, eyes black against green shadow,
but your exact curve and shade is hidden from me.
I can only guess at what you fear you would be losing.

I want to unbutton my cotton shirt and say,
look, mine are odd too, my right breast so much larger.
I want to touch your breast for comfort, or hold you,
but I can not. I can not even say that we are friends.

With me you are intimate and distant
like a grackle that passes glittering in the winter sun,
veers, and leaves her shadow briefly on the grass.
You are cautious about how near you get to me
and though I practice the patience of grass
I do not wait for our embrace.

1980

WHAT HAPPENED YEARS AGO

for S. W.

Yes, it is nine years later, this month,

and yes, I sent the postcard, no return address,
because of what happened years ago. Did you
send it like a paper plane into the trash?

a piece of sentimental debris: starfish, blue
ocean, clear sand: no plastic cup, no salt
bitterness, no dead fish, bones in confusion.

No, I don't think of you simply: even to walk
the beach with you was elaborate:
the glitter of sand on your feet, the gawk

of sunbathers at two such women, and me desperate
to watch the long harsh bones of your feet
taken in the hand of the water. Did you hate

me in the end? do you? do my words again steal
your life? You were my life. *Oh*
words, words, you say, your voice cruel.

Yes, the voice is my imagining, echo
in a hollow room we both have left.
I saw the place last week, five miles below,

waves fixed as a pattern in a carpet.
In ten minutes my flight traversed
the beach, Wilmington, the river, all flat

as a paper diagram, neutral of the urgent
love I had for you there.
It was true: between us nothing, no movement.

But what about this? I have, in a drawer,
your pair of yellow glittery socks
which, sometimes, for comfort, I wear,

despite the ragged heels. In your thoughts
do you sometimes hold me in brief carelessness?

1984

NOT A GUN, NOT A KNIFE

for C.S.

I don't want this to be happening again, and to you.

Your bruised voice over the phone: *In the bathroom: this*
doesn't get easier to say: raped. And your throat choked
on sperm.
                    The words get harder for me to write since the poem
that I gave after your first rape did not work as a lock,

did not bite like a dog when the man shoved
his fingers through your latched screen door and forced
you.
        Of what use this paper of words: not a gun,
not a knife, not the muscle of club by your bed,

not the flimsy surface of my shoulder for you to rest on,
not even the skin of a love letter like those I once wrote you.

But I send it, because this is what I have to give you,
because I know you: smart-handed: can put any scrap to use:

maybe this to be crumpled like kleenex, distraction
or company for your hand if you are crying: maybe

flipped to the blank side for a typed list of curses,
then burned, clean sulphur, ashes fraying:

maybe the page turned to this description: how steadily you
brush at your pale hair in the bathroom, ready to go out

to the bar, talk about nothing much with the women
drinking beer by the pool table, put your quarter down,

twist the blue chalk with tensile fingers against the cue.

1983

YOUR VOICE HAS CARRIED ME

for B.D.

Just a few words, Barbara: since I am afraid
you are tired, or in the circle of suffering
as before: the pain a thousand repetitive voices.

Your voice has carried me (and if me, how many?)
up from the island afternoon heat, thermal,
as much spiral as the great bronze-black birds
over the fish dumps, the bones, the fish themselves
pink-scaled in aquamarine channels, the water
extended into the sky,
                                        your hand showing
the way that a gesture of love moves from the one
at your side, through the horizon,
                                                        your hand
that fed me at supper the tender cheek of fish
sweet from next the covered expressive eye.

I wish these words as sweet, or at least clever
as a magic fish bone, the kind you hold in your mouth
and instantly swim wherever you want in the world,

so you could be home, if you wanted, in the channel
floating like the octopus in your rubbery black suit,
or sitting in your front room in noon air
hot as the Gulf beach, shallow salt water.

Not so clever, Barbara, but strong love I return
to you (with that of the many others), a current
for the pull of your muscular spirit, the wing-
or fin-beat, to take you where you want to be.

1984

FOR A STUDENT

You say you're a woman but have never experienced
oppression. Can I ask: do you own a car? Ever drive
around aimlessly? So much depends on point-of-view,
and the ability to enter a situation and then leave
if you're not interested. If you've got the gas, the oil,
tires, and no red diamond of a failed inspection
stuck on the windshield.
What's this got to do with women?
Well, I drive out sometimes, like you? not to shop but
to try on the day like a new blue blouse with white embroidery.
Yesterday I was in a neighborhood not mine when

the traffic thickens at an obstruction and I stop.
Past the red light, a woman is having a vision, naked.
She stands in the street dirt at a sawhorse barricade,
feet gleaming as if just stepped from water,
shoes beside her sloughed off like black scuffed shells.
The light of her brown body shines splendidly back at the sun.
She beckons power to her, hands over head: in Spanish
she requests, in English she vows love to an infinite you.
She declares what need brings her to this mundane place.

Her closed eyes never turn to the policeman calling
softly into his walkie-talkie, or the one tying
a fluid blue-green dress around her neck. Her cunt,
before it is hidden, looks at me, a third eye,
symmetrical brown triangle. The shape and color
mine exactly. We could be sisters by the resemblance.

Everyone looks. She is the child's nightmare of shame.
She is a hidden self in the stark daylight. I pull
excuses around me: I don't understand her language;
they won't believe we're kin. As I drive by, I look

and look away, her beauty terror to me. I do not see
what happens next to the one who asks more than clothes,
the woman, caught in the choke of traffic, demanding love.

In the building behind her, construction workers look
out of empty window sockets, and the pit they've made
stares up out of the crumpled lawns of ruined apartments.
Going to school girls wink in the harsh corner light.
In the dirt the round green eyes of broken bottles blink.
People out of work under the chinaberry trees
draw and throw down cards marked with red and black eyes.
Everyone is looking; no one is stopping their business,
and I drive through the intersection.

You say, perhaps,
an experience that doesn't happen everyday: yet it does.
In the obscurity of a back downstairs room I have raved
close to her. Someday so might you. There is a secret voice
shouting dangers and answers, not yet lost, despite our skin
like a white Sunday dress that conceals the disreputable cunt,
despite hurrying through unfamiliar streets in the car,
windows rolled up, radio turned up, FM 93.9, WKYS.

1985

READING MAPS: TWO

for Mab

I have no map for the past, for going home to see
my mother, on the back roads between Opelika and Clanton,
on toward evening. This year she is seventy,
I am thirty-five, grownup but still her child.
We love each other, but she doesn't talk to me much,
not the secret words of the heart, her struggle to be
a good woman for twice as long as I have lived.

I have heard proverbs from her: *a whistling woman,*
a crowing hen, always come to a bad end.
About her life, mostly silence, a blank piece of paper.
I want to rip that up, useless guide to this land
we were both born and raised in, the place I drive through
now, over the Tallapoosa, the Coosa, over roads made
on dirt paths once marked by Choctaws with painted trees,
past fields where, within her lifetime, good Christian men
made bonfires, burned Black folk like pine, while the women
lifted up the children to see.
What does she know
that she has not told me? memories locked in her heart
like letters in the cedar chest, words faded to brown ink,
memories like old newspapers piled in the garage,
headlines black on brittle paper.

When I was twelve,
I went through bureau drawers looking for my mother,
opened a leather diary, written before she married. The brown ink
curved like her voice. The few lines I saw,
never spoken, doubted my father. When she saw me,
she said nothing. Later she took her words behind the garage
and tore them page by page into a wire wastebasket
and burned them, flames orange as daylilies in the yard.
The pages flared open, shrivelled, twisted, then dropped
to ashes on the ground.

I want her to tell me
she doubted them, the men, the women, who taught her
to live with things the way they were. I want to know
if sometimes she veered from the road she was told to take:

the way she drove her father to Bessemer, the steel mill,
the year she was sixteen, every week left him,
picked him up. He was a security guard,
she said she didn't know exactly what he did.
This year I figured out: that was about when
T.C.I. hired white men with shotguns to walk the fence,
noose of barb wire around people in its company towns,
to lock iron on the feet of Black men, prisoners leased
from the state.

I don't know exactly what he did.
I wanted her to know, and knowing, to have held
herself separate from him. She has always tried
to do the right thing. I don't know exactly what she did.

I want her to be company for me tonight, on the road
fifteen miles from home, for her to give me a way to live,
not this puzzle of why she and the women I call kin
chose the ways they did.

I don't want to be left
alone in this place, once familiar as my own body,
where now the ground heaves around me with secrets
my mother never knew or never told me. I don't want
to be left here trying to find my way by guess and memory.

Silent lightning strikes the road ahead, splits
the pink and yellow sky like a peach into halves,
like a peach off one of Mr. Randolph's trees
that I ate as it lay, warm as a small sun, in my hands.
The road narrows between sides of red clay,
almost the road I climbed up in the afternoons, the dirt
gullied, crumbling around roots snaked out from trees,
the stubborn clay that I saw remake itself
into hill, even as it was worn away.

With the lightning and thunder of rain the road turns
slick as hard clay I once stood on and slid
the storm between my feet, felt the downpour
quick and free as a creek over my naked skin.

In the headlights' glare the road turns to steam.
Sudden wind flops the trash, the plastic bags
on the edge of dirt. Out of the corner of my eye I see
them. They are bodies convulsing, stirring in the ground

by the side of the same road that once took me further south,
toward Meridian, to my greataunt's, to my grandmother's house,
where I sat on the porch by day and watched the road,
how the white dust stirred hot around
the feet of Black women and men, how they turned
off on a path I did not know through the woods.

On moonless nights, when the woods came right up to the porch,
when the chuck-will's-widow spoke out of miles of dark,
I sat safe on the other side of the screen with the women
in my family. We never talked about what went on in the night
unless one of the neighbors, come over with deer meat, told
about a hunt, how he and other men shined lights
in wild eyes, made a wall of glare, shot
the animal as it paused to choose a path back
into the woods.

During the day we didn't mention
how the road from Mobile and Jackson, from Montgomery,
Birmingham, connected to our road, or how
that road became the path that went behind the house,
wore down the grass to the backyard where a Black woman
did our wash in an iron pot over a slow fire.

I want to drive into the past now and ask the women
in my family what they thought about what they saw
from the porch, if they thought about what they didn't see
the years they hooked rugs there, knitted and tatted,
quilted, silently uttered their comforts. Then
I didn't question them; I watched white cotton
thread unroll from between their fingers, present become
future in rows as patterned as tracks in the white sand.

I wanted to be like them, with hands that could speak
stitch by stitch, make something out of nothing,
have a house with a porch where men never sat,
have an island of shade at the edge of sunlight,
the glare netted by clematis vines on the screen,
hear no sound but bees or a louder hum,
the red-throated hummingbird's wings; sit safe
at the edge of night, the porch a stretch of yellow haze
under the naked electric bulb, buzzes,
junebugs stopped by the screen, the mesh of light;
to live quiet and sometimes work puzzles on the card table
with the other women, match jigsaws of color,
out of a thousand pieces make a landscape,
wheat fields under purple clouds, a woman
bending with a scythe in a foreign countryside.

I wanted to be like them and I was: in the afternoons
I watched from the porch as the cornfields stretched
green as a yard around me, and the road that ran past,
glittering, white, was our road.

I did not see
the hidden road, the one made in the dark blue sands,
the grey, brown, yellow red sands, the river sands
on the shore of an ancient sea;
the one made
by the feet of Choctaw people walking from the Tombigbee
to the mound of the great mother, walking to the west
with the little cry *yaiya ishkitini*, with the big cry
yaiya chito, driven out of their woods;
the road
made by the feet of Ibo people stolen
from the land where they hoed their sweet yams, beans,
walking to chop cotton in strange fields at dawn;

the road of their children's children, Black women,
Q.T. or Dinah, who came up to clean house,
wash or cook, get Aunt Janie up or put her
to bed, smooth her arthritic legs, then go down

the road just before dark, down the white thread of sand,
walking home to houses we didn't see from the porch.

I have wanted to be like the women in my family and I am,
even lately when I don't want to be:
                                                            I have
the look of Mary when she sat her horse over fields
rowed green with corn, black with fifteen slaves,
all grist for her mill in the bend of the river
where the road crossed over on her ferry.
                                                                    I know
I take after Mary Jane who lived her life
inside the fine-toothed shade of black walnuts
on land bountied to her husband for murder of the Creeks,
who died as she nursed her eldest grandson, caught
in the bed in mosquito netting on fire, a gauze
of flame.
                    I know I have the ways of Lethe Ann
whose road ran between the house, the turkey pen,
and church, her eyes fixed on the cross.
                                                                    And I am like
my grandmother who never knew who her mother was,
brought home birth-red by her father, riding
down the river road, the tracks leading back
to Perry County, but his words never to the woman
at the fork of whose legs she began her journey.

Tonight if I followed this road, the unwinding grey thread,
to each of them, to their graves, if I knelt in the grass,
the dew cold on my hands, to tell them I want
to alter the pattern we were born into, to ask them
to help me, to show me the hidden ways
that they used to change how things were, I am afraid
each voice would sound in the night air, sweet
as cape jessamine, like the only voice that I have
recorded, Ora's that spins off the tape
naming my grandsires, not a word of herself except
that she and sister Laura took their fortunes from *Proverbs:*
thirty-one, thirteen: *She worketh willingly with her hands.*
I know when she tacked bits of cloth together
everywhichway, made a pattern as she pleased,

cotton from chickenfeed sacks, wool
from old coats, she called that quilt *crazy*.

If I follow this road tonight, I will come
to my mother's house. I have wanted her to tell me
how to live. I have no record of her work:
the twenty years of weekly trips out in the county,
the visits to women with children that had to be fed,
the magazines to women trying to teach themselves to read,
sitting with Mattie who had worked all her life in the fields,
who prophesied a different world, no more death, no sorrow,
all tears wiped from their eyes.
                                                  She wrote down
office records, directions for the red tangled roads,
where to turn left at the pine tree, at the sign
Jesus Saves. I don't know where she stopped,
where sometimes she went further on, or
how she felt as she sat on the porches of the women,
if from there death and sorrow ever looked
like the white men at the courthouse, or herself,
or if she saw how she resembled the woman opposite.

I resemble her, just as when I sat between her legs
in the bath, the water wide as a creek around us.
We were together but separate. I have wanted us to be
separate, like islands in the bend of the river, apart
from the land we live in, different from how we have been,
and together.

                        But when I told her I had left my husband,
was departing from the way things were, when I said
the hidden word *lesbian*, she wanted to hear no more
in this life, not a word to her people. She saw silence
between us, in the hereafter: I would burn like the woods
on fire in September.

                                    I remembered fever as a child,
yellow walls of my room like a sandy road in noon sun,
the bed in flames, my mother at the door. I can not
remember if she came to me or if she walked away.

1982

for Joan

FIRST NIGHT

You tell me you notice light always,
its slant, its shift, how it touches
surface, how it becomes shadow.

You say you want to see me, but not
naked under the light's harsh glare,
nor do you want to lie down in the dark.

You shade the lamp beside us with cloth.
The room shifts: water below sunned surface.
You direct the light to fall over my skin

as delicately as you touch my shadowed side.

7/17/1981

WHEN I CALL YOUR NAME

July is over, four hot weeks
Of August, two long weeks in September,
And then I'll be in your bedroom, in your bed,
Nibbling your pink earlobe.

Even in the city, our day will be
Luscious, your hair black and twining
In my hands like the wild muscadine grape.
Scuppernong brown, your nipples will be full
Against my mouth. We will look through
Barred windows at night for the harvest moon.
Equinox soon will diminish the light.
Tell me, love, how to speed time now,
How to slow it then, when I call your name.

8/5/1981

WINGED SEEDS

If you were here, we would sit and hold hands
  on the back steps. The humming bird
    would come to feed in the vines
      of red trumpet flower,
        hover dance,
        wings gauze,
      push her white throat
    into each open bloom. Fearless
  and greedy, she would dispute nectar
with a wasp. We would drink ice tea and kiss.

If I were there, you would hum in my ear and dance
  with me in the kitchen, like the wind outside
    in the winged maple seeds. Our hands
      would mingle, lead us to bed,
        open curtains,
        touch breeze,
      stirring cool over our skin.
    Under the star of your quilt, our knees
  together, we would whirl, listen to the wind
that we bring into the room to hum to us as we kiss.

8/23/1981

CABBAGE MOON

I missed you tonight. I had gone out
just before dark to the garden to cut
what was left of the cabbages. In the hollows
of red clay there was rain and freezing.
In the middle of the trumpet vines by the fence
a wind hummed and tongued. I was satisfied
to be alone under the curve of a deep
blue night that emptied the last
daylight into the west behind me.
I was content to squat down in the dirt
with a kitchen knife, cut each knot
of stem, gather the cabbages up
in my arms, their fragile full breasts
against mine. I did not miss you
until I stood to go. Then I saw
at the edge of the pasture the swell
of the moon, her rapid rise to face me
full, the splendor of her eye on mine.

Then I remembered: when you come close
the world becomes a room for us to embrace in.
I felt your breath warm the back of my neck,
your breasts heavy against the width of my back.
In the winter garden your hands gathered mine.

But the moon showed me by her light only
my shadow lying across the icy ground.

1/9/1982

DARNING NEEDLE

After you were sad, after our hands veered,
dipped to touch the other's skin, like swallows
at dusk over the surface of water, iridescent,
ecstatic, after we slept close as two wings
folded together in the night, I was happy the next day
when you said you had seen your heart being mended
with strong, uneven stitches, a binding thread
left as if a silver invisible needle had darted
in and out over the torn surface, like a dragon-
fly skims the pond, darns the water
with the trail of her eggs, like the nymph's skin grows,
cracks, expands again, until she splits into herself
in flight, like her many-faceted eye breaks
the water in ten thousand thousand glitters,
yet holds the world, earth to air, she between.

2/3/1982

IN A SOLITARY PLACE

I was going to write to you about romance:
since I have thought it a mirage, to love another
out of need, to let an angle of light, some distance,
old thirsts, spill her, a pool of water on the horizon;

since I have loved you and, as we neared, as illusions
dispersed, begun to see what I had not noticed
or had not imagined, the flame, emerald green, flashed
by the sun just after it sets, just before it rises.

But tonight the continent stretches between us,
flat grey sand. I haven't touched you in weeks,
won't be able to for more, have been in meetings
all day with others who are depressed, drunk three cups
of coffee, half a glass of beer, touched myself roughly,
come with salt bitter tears, don't feel hopeful.

I want to be glad now in my solitary place,
to be able to call up green grass from my day's desert.
I know your absence does not keep me from this, but I know
your glance and hand would be for me lightning at night.

2/23/1982

IN EACH OTHER'S ARMS, LIGHTNING

When we sat on the bed and spoke as if across
a fence, you said: *I think we fight*
like this because we can't see each other's face.
We were in the dark. The yellow candles, flowers,
forsythia, burned on the mantle in the other room.

This morning, it's blue outside. I am hoeing
in the garden, rows for onions, spinach,
sunflowers. The sun has burned my neck
red as I flush when I want you, with your hand
against my back, just below my shoulderblades
as if we were dancing, but to move me
closer, my stomach against yours, hot
as my hands in the red dirt of the garden.

It's close to noon. We could lie down
in the dirt. Our faces would be plain in the sun,
no shadows. We could see again how alike
and how different we are, like our breasts. But

I am afraid that even in the open, suddenly
we might look too far, too close. With a move
or a word, we are in the storm. I see
you leave me, your face change
like clouds that rush up from heated land
toward thunder. You see me move
away from you, my face shift
abrupt, sun to shade, as a field turns
into another place under rapid clouds.

Then I can't remember when I met you
or believe that you'll touch me again.
I want to leave you for somewhere
safe. I go inside myself like a house,

close my heart and my face. For you
to be able to see that I want you
across a space you've made is dangerous,
your love a blade of heat lightning.
For me to see you look across
a distance I have caused is despair
heavy as water in the air before the storm
breaks.

Then I think it will be us
to shatter. Yet always there is a move
or a word, and I remember that I love you,
how you love me, the way we tremble
and flicker in each other's arms, lightning.

It's close to noon. If we sat in the sun
we would look ordinary as dirt, not like the times
we consume each other almost to ashes.
Under my rolled-up sleeve, on my upper arm,
I have a small yellow bruise, left
from when we last held each other.
It will fade soon.

I don't want you to leave me.
I want something to hold to, to remind me
you'll stay, like the grey ashes from the woodstove
I scatter by hand in the garden.

4/9/1982

FIRST YEAR

Or if we count by nights: a hundred and one,
some as fabulous as a fairy tale, the rare kisses,
the what we did with our tongues, the adventures at hand,
the rough soft passage through cliffs of our bodies.

Or should we count by miles? thousands, enough
for three continents, to be in the same room talking,
to compass the other by voice and touch, to meet
by river, by ocean, by island, by mangrove swamp.

Or I could count by sounds: teeth of rain
against our window, mouth of blue lightnings, you saying
come in my ear, tongue of vulva on my thigh,
the night trains that we hear moan, late, as we sleep

stayed in each other's arms, between how long
we have been together, how we are yet to be.

6/4/1982

AN ACT INEXPLICABLE BY THEORY

Why do we love each other? curiosity? stubbornness?
Before we kiss, we do not say: *Cultural differences,*
or: *We defy history,* when we make love and come
to the place outside time where our skins kiss,
there at my stiff Scot ribs, your *zaftig* belly.

But time comes that we lie bitter, together,
apart, in bed:
                    on nights when time bites me
with iron teeth, the clasp of chastity belt
on my filthy vulva, the *camisole de force* to hold me
pure, even now, by will of the lord of crusades;

on nights when time rolls over you like a yellow wheel,
circle of cloth over your heart, medieval *rouelle*
to turn you out as filthy, as Jew, set apart;

on nights when you are my sin, centuries of fear
in a second, contagion, to touch will turn me
beast, my body gnaw my soul to nothing;

on nights when I am your betrayal, this week in Paris,
the gunman at breakfast because it was an ordinary Jewish
restaurant, when it is your blood on the tablecloth;

and us in bed, side by side, ourselves
and our bodies of myth and history, when it is
your danger or abandonment, my despair and self-hatred,
when this difference joins the others between us,
chain links in a fence, and we see each other
from opposite sides,
                              yet each time our hands
reach through, an act inexplicable by theory.

9/1/1982

STUBBORN AS A YEAR AGO

I have thistles in my house in a blue bottle
on my bookcase. They remind me of how we love.
This afternoon everything reminds me, but
at the moment it is thistles, in particular,

with their winged spiny stems, their flowers
become white hair, flying.
                                        On Sunday I'll be thirty-six,
stubborn as a year ago: you can't touch
sometimes, it's like grabbing knives. I know,

like you. And the way I admire your grey hairs,
you count mine: perhaps new lovers always talk
of growing old together, wild and old.
I think we will, even if our hands have scars.

I know I've told you this before. But this minute
thistledown in the air was your hair, my breath.

9/7/1982

BLUEBERRIES

Love, I know you well: how you look, desiring,
upper lip lengthened when you look at what you
want: some wet fat blueberries heaped in bowls, or
me, at times, wet too.

10/9/1982

THE EYE OF ONE WHO LOVES YOU

Late afternoon: sunlight deflected pink
into the room from the red brick wall opposite:
a flush of light on your face and breasts: you look
like you do after we've made love.

I hold your hand and say: *You are beautiful.*
I want to hold the words like a mirror before you
so you will see: how your hair this moment stirs
dark, silver, luminous around your head; the quirks

cleverly turned by your ear and nose; the veer
of wrinkles, the passion around your eyes; desire
under your eyes, shadows; how in your eyes reside
powers of love and curiosity, your outrageous life.

You say: *This is not the image reflected in my mirror.*
I ask: *Has that been the eye of one who loves you?*

10/9/1982

WATER AND EARTH

We have called our love *transformation,*
the promise of something shaped differently,
more beautifully, in us, between us, and in the world,
to know where power lies rigid between us,
to change by a love that pours out like water,
like rain falling in the garden, that seeps
down to the roots and speaks to them
of fatness and growth.
                                        Today what I remember
of our last visit is:
                                how I cried the first days
when you were strange to me, how my heart,
my stomach, my lungs turned to water and poured
hot from my eyes, how I sat in the bath, crying,
grief panting out of my mouth, like steam from the water,

how some nights we read together, elaborate stories
of women lovers who bury and dig each other up
for love, how we laughed as we recognized ourselves,

how in the end you held my head as we talked,
your hand deep in my hair at the roots, tenderly
following the shape of my head.
                                                        On the phone
you said of the visit, you were happier because
I had loved you. I had loved you, and
you had loved me, and today I saw myself
sitting on your couch (was it raining that day?)
my throat swelled with grief, pain behind my tongue,
how it burst from the base of my throat and poured
like blood, like water, not words, on the floor.

Yesterday I read a poet who wrote that once
she scalded her hand with a spout of boiling water

out of grief and rage from love; she called that
self-mutilation: it left pink scars on her wrist.

We have called love *transformation.* I have thought
of the pain as growing pains, my womb clenched,
laboring, after my water broke, drenching me.

12/6/1982

BURY AND DIG

We bury and dig each other up
for love. Sometimes it's like death,
sometimes like carrots: invisible
seeds delicately smoothed under,
a slow growth, filaments of hair
at the root; grasping, pulling
at more hair, springy and leafy,
the cool length of your thigh,
a smell of red dirt under my nails.

Sometimes like beets: wintering over
under ground, the red heart waiting.

12/11/1982

IT WILL ALWAYS BE TOO SOON

Breaking up   breaking up   we talked
all those hours about breaking up:
                                                  facing
on the couch, your feet in my hands like cup-and-saucer,
or in bed, my ass to your stomach, like spoons.

All that talk, so I didn't write your poem
for the feast of lights. It was to be about
different kinds of light and you and me:
                                                            the balcony,
moonlight wet as water on your skin, bluecrabs
running sideways on the beach, how you slid me
through your hands:
                                    where we pushed up against the wall,
kissing, the flecks of paint loosened, glittering
like mica in the sun the next day.
                                                  The other lights,
the other poem didn't get written:
                                                  we were talking
about breaking up:
                                  for long moments my body felt
like a place where nights were long as days,
a continent of ice breaking into fragments, floating
far from you.

                    But do you know how I'd know
we were really breaking up?
                                            I would stop
wanting to write poems for you:
                                                and I wouldn't
let myself remember how we lit the candles
every night, when the mirror held us together,
troubled or easy, your face, my face, our hands
glowing over the small flames, the brief shared ceremony:

the way I remember you, just before we sleep
at night, leaning toward the candle: when your mouth
gathers the breath of the world, when your face holds
light in the world, and shadow: the sun, the moon,
desires of my heart: with one breath, darkness in the room,
but always too soon, too soon, for my eyes.

12/23/1982

STAYING TOGETHER

Do you know why I think we stay together?

Because we fight in the car on the Beltway,
first about doing our clothes in a Rockville laundrymat,
then about everything: closeness, farness, love;
you mad enough to drive into an abutment,
me mad enough to open my door and jump;
both yelling, crying, past the Mormon Temple
lit like a Disney spaceship, which makes me
feel worse, like we're on the wrong planet.

After we both say, in different, loud frenzy:
How can anything be worth this? silence for twenty
minutes, the brief repeated glare of mile markers.
Then you ask in a mouselike voice if I would like
to go get in a hot tub with you, and I laugh.

12/23/1982

WE SAY WE LOVE EACH OTHER

You say: *The trouble is: we don't understand*
each other.
                    Your sounds have fascinated me
from the first, the way you laugh in your throat
like a saxophone. But last time the radio played
reedy brass, low sexy, I started crying
(last time, in the car alone, Duke Street,
the aroma of tobacco curing, invisible smoke
in my mouth, small jazz being played in a room
in a distant city).
                              Lately I understand this:
I want your voice, mysterious music of your body,
yet our words, gestures are from different
languages.
                    If we are sitting on the couch, eating
oranges, sweet acid, like lovemaking,
                                                  and the phone
rings in another room:
                                        you answer, you murmur,
my stomach vibrates, a deep drum flutter at your sound:

you come back, I do not ask *Who was it?*
to me, intrusion, a push into your room:
to you, removal, uncaring of closeness:

then we are sitting on the couch, abrupt
separate. The bitter orange rinds sit
in a neat pile on the round dish before us.

I am sitting in a place made for me
by women, generations, Scot, Irish, sitting
on a little bit of land, holding on,
survival on an island, isolation, a closed mouth
in their own kitchen, self-containment.

You are sitting in a place made for you
by women, generations, Jews in Spain, Holland,
Russia, the Pale, Poland, Roumania, America,
the pogroms, no bit of land safe, none
to be owned as home, survival by asking, asking,
knowing where every one was, enemy, family.

Later if we talk about this moment, we observe,
abstract. Even as I write, I make it distant

but we are sitting on the couch: separate, not abstract.
History speaks like a voice through our bodies:
how often we do not know that it is this we do not
understand.
                    Fascination with what we have not known:
your hand gripping my chin, drawing me to your mouth;
my interest in a yellow gingko leaf, in veins
in my palm, my look up, the sudden kiss I give you.

What we fight bitterly: voices scraping against
demanding, selfish.
                              Where is the future we spoke of,
between us, stronger by difference?

                                                  We sit on the couch
trying to understand each other:
                                             lists, signs, point
to an object, give words, *what do you mean?*
                                                            paper
with pictures, paper with words, poems, photographs,
repeating, explaining, exasperation, anger,
                                                          asking
what did you mean?
                               The other says she loves: how believe
when her words, her gestures are not the ones that speak
love to you?
                    We sit on the couch. You rub my feet:
my heels are small oval drums. The radio plays
something we can't dance to. The room smells of oranges.
After a while, we say again we love each other.

1/8/1983

I ADMIT THE NEED

Today has come to this: night, me alone
in bed, my stomach wanting weight and more warmth
against it than two blankets,
                                        my day's doings
stuck between the pages of my book, slips of paper
next to the raw-handed struggle, poverty,
Daughter of the Earth who walled herself against
love and tenderness that menace the freedom of women.

I have struggled against you: to love was weakness,
betrayal of the hard-won self. Tonight I admit
the need: to lie beside you in common struggle,
at your side's warmth to repeat the day's efforts,
no matter how small:
                                that I talked to a friend
about the weary distance to you, my plans to move,
but her anger and fears were hands push-pulling
at me:
            that I fought a mechanic about the brakes,
the bill, half a month's living:
                                        that I bought
for my neighbor a few pleasures, canned milk,
a small jar of oysters, juicy as tongues,
some crackers, a thumb-sized green can of snuff:

that I fetched her kerosene, two five-gallon cans
from the Salvation Army, that I heard her shouting
later at spirit companions who would not come:

that I was too afraid of being alone to work,
that I wanted to talk to you, that I fell asleep
wanting you to lie on me, your breasts and thighs
on me like a heavy blanket:
                                        that in the night

I dreamed: your voice in my ear like a telephone call,
my stutter of fear, my room stretched out from the bed
vast, empty, or if someone leaned from the shadows,
it wasn't you, who grew impatient with my inability to speak.

1/12/1983

NIGHT GIVES US THE NEXT DAY

Tonight it is raining ice, no thunder, no light-
ning, just the cold rain hissing in the leaves.
Things are growing a skin of ice. Come close.
Warm my skin with the palm of your hand. I don't want
us brittle cold with pain. I want to dance
the flamingo with you, hot pink, and kiss.

The night weather is changeable as us: a kiss
of ice, then thunder, now melting rain, light
tongues whispering in the air: will we dance?
will we fight? You tell me of a lover who leaves
you: you won't leave me. But I've felt your want
change, shut tight against me, felt your heart close.

And me? Yes, I'm one afraid to be close.
I've said so. Have I said I'm afraid to lose one kiss
of yours? I've known how I'd love if I let myself want.
This is what I want: to be with you in slant light,
shifting weather, morning, evening, forever: neither leaves
the other: so unlikely. But will you save a dance?

and we could do the duck, the raccoon, the fish: dance
thighs pressed against cunts: absolutely too close
for public. But not for the bar: The Other Side leaves
the lights down low: we could do more than kiss,
oh yes, we could practice who leads, how a light
hand, a supple back lead wherever they want:

to the car, to make out, make love, drive if we want,
midnight to the coast, hear the rain's uneven dance
in the marshes at dawn by Pamlico Sound: light
no fire, but watch in the grey, huddled close,
for flocks of islands, the wintering ducks: kiss
at the clap of their wings: thunder and night leaves:

leaves us together, not waked from a dream: leaves
us the next day, the days after. Say that's what you want.
There's still 15th Street, where we managed to kiss
in a grey drift of tear gas: we've yet to dance
there: or the streets where women must pull blankets close,
sleep on islands of steam, to live through to light.

Tonight rain in the street leaves cold hope that the women will dance.
But we've worked more than change in the weather by stubborn want. Close
your arms around me, kiss me. We'll tell secrets on the world until light.

2/8/1983

YOUR HAND OPENS ME

Flat on our backs on the floor, boards hard as packed clay:

I've wanted to make love with you outside, your ass
sunk into a curve of dirt, my fingers sunk in you
up to the knuckles and palm: your hips, my feet
thrashing the leaves like some unknown animal just
out of sight in the bushes.
                                        Not tonight: we are quiet,
behind a door, away from the cold, the other women:

quiet, your hand opening, opening me, to the width
of light made by one candle, opening my thighs
clenched against the night, an eye pressed up to the window,
someone who might look at my secret.
                                                            I need
your hand moving in me, unpredictable hot fingers:
my throat opens, my mouth closes on sounds,
high, stretched, squeals as the swifts fall
in the chimney, jostled from their night roosts, thumping
behind the bricks: like my heels on the floor.

                                                                        Sometimes
I'm afraid: when we make love or I write like this:
my need for you: that you'll look at me from the outside,
through the blank windows and think *how ridiculous:* a woman
with face opened to a throat, words nothing but
squeal and thump.

                              I have been afraid: you have held me,
tonight your right arm between me and the harsh dusty floor,
your left hand pressing me open, praising my secrets.

You have loved me: so I can come to you again
like this: my need for you naked as me,
flat on my back, thighs open, against the boards.

6/19/1983

PEACH

My tongue, your ass:
the center of a peach,
ripe, soft, pitted, red-fibred flesh,
dissolving toward earth, lust.
Eat you? I ask.

7/18/1983

PLUMS

I love the way you
give me cold plums. I love the
way you give me tongues.

7/18/1983

LIVING IN A POSTCARD

Out my fifth story window the Capitol dome sits up,
spotlit bald, like tonight painted behind a Senator
in a TV studio, like a Greetings-from-D.C. postcard,

except I'm in it, and the dogs howling in the yard,
scraped dirt below, and Ida yelling in the alley, forgetting
each word as she utters it, on her way for more wine.

I'm in it, and the blue-pink hydrangeas by moonlight,
by the cool iron back steps where someone is sitting,
shadowy, another neighbor of the hundreds I do not know.

I'm in it, and so are you, kissing me in front of the window,
so that the dome glows like a breast in the close distance.
But in an hour, unlike the moon, it will not have changed.

What happens if we stand at the front of the postcard?

as we did one night, last month, in front of the White House,
the blood-red flowers, the iron bars, the desperate sign
Wanted: Wisdom and Honesty. By our candle's stare

we read out loud the words of a heart that knew its war
forty years ago, a poem that said *believe and resist*
forever: that said *Jew, Negro, labor, red,*

woman: but did not say *lesbian*. There we stood:
while to our left a man photographed himself, with friends,
smiling, up close to the fence and the opulent lawn:

to our right a bearded man listened until the word *woman*:
he walked away then. And then the poem ended, and
we walked off holding hands. No siren howled, just the tap,

the knock of the words, on a closed door. What had changed?

But I felt the heavy air divide around our bodies as we walked.
That's why I love you: the years you've made the world
rearrange itself around the fact of *lesbian*: the years

you've made photographs that show the moment, limber
as light, when we walk from present into future, the change
that follows us like a shadow across the ground, unnoticed:

the picture, queers massed in the street, roller-
skating away from the Capitol; the picture, us
in my bedroom, the window fan a turning metal flower;

your postcard of two women touching, taped to a refrigerator
door, McGhee's Crossroads, so a woman there can know
she is not the only one: the belief that brought us,

midnight, to the hot guarded street: together, stubborn.

7/13/1983

THE NAPE OF YOUR NECK

When I came back into the restaurant, it was as
I had left it: a salesman, two travelling families
at the brown formica tables, a plastic rack of salt,
anonymous sugar, spoons, a stand of rubber philodendron,
you at the corner table, head bent over a map.

Your head bent, the nape of your neck exposed,
browner than your belly but not the back of your hands.

Outside, the lines on the map are roads, the turnpike
through Ohio, layers of asphalt, forgotten dirt,
dying trees, acid beading like rain in the foliage.

I smelled water only once this morning, a low spot,
the green smell of growth, where dirt and water mix
with the mumble of things beginning. This used to be
the smell of where I lived. Now it is your smell,

your head bent over the map, the smell at the nape
of your neck, the sweat, the smell between your legs.

If you turned your head now, you might be a stranger:
the separation, our anger. From the door I see: nowhere
and you, whose look can call me home in a room
of strangers, where the only sound is the nape of your neck.

8/20/1983

USUALLY WE ARE NOT FOOLED BY DESPAIR

So everyone asks *what do you think of Washington*?

This week suddenly it is where the spinning bomb will drop.

Out of my window at sunset suddenly screams from each row house
open window, between silver iron bars, marigolds: usually no sounds:
or a party, Joan Armatrading: or tambourines, praying:

now it's the town screaming.
In one heartbeat, the sky will flash
the end: when I blink, the sky will come in my window and eat me.

But I can see that the dome of the Capitol glows unvaporized
in the long orange light.
Its men did a week's work moving
MX missiles like checkers on the map: are home watching TV football.
Thirty-three seconds left! they are screaming with my neighbors
as the local team wins.

So I ask myself *how do*
you like Washington?
looking down Maryland Avenue on the grid,
spoke of the wheel to the hub, the dome poking up:
the hill
on the grid of mutually assured destruction where I live now
near you:
sleep with you in my bed every other night, my skin
lapping quietly at yours like a tongue: below us the dome
never blinks over the white of its lit sleepless eye:
in the morning
we drink black tea with milk: the sun goes down the streets
between houses, creek between rocks, shiny rooftops: the dome
a white cloud that does not move.

If the end comes you say
suddenly *I hope I am with you like this.*
I see us from a distance
like a movie except the panorama shifts:
it is the town in the fifties
where you were left to die with your mother, the times your father went
to live inside a secret mountain dome of rock:
it could be the town
I grew up in, the courthouse reared up in the middle, my father
at his desk inside, inside his skin like pale metal, his white fear
annihilation.

But usually we are not fooled by despair,
not even when a helicopter whacks the air with spinning knives
just above my roof: when it returns again, again
with its bulging eye: when we know the police are hunting for
someone.
Even then, with you I can believe a possible future
with the domed hub unable to spin the world around it: and sudden
lively vertigo when people in millions push at the rim.
Harder
to imagine exactly how to move my fear.

At the slow end
of the day I walk my street. There is a yard, small, diagonal,
outlandish in a row of regimented lawns. A Black woman has set out
painted rocks asymmetrically, chlorox bottles with marigolds
and pink touch-me-nots. She has stuck silverblue delicate pinwheels,
plastic windmills, in the bushes. They click like tambourines,
like mouths; they dilate and close, pupils of eyes. It is all
hurly-burly, topsy-turvy, vertigo: hope: the world imagined new.

10/23/1983

THE FACT OF THE GARDEN

With this rain I am satisfied we will be together
in the spring. Seeds of water on my window glass,
transparent sprouts and rootlets; in your backyard
steady rain through the heavy dirt we dug in,
our shovels excavating some history of the tiny garden.

Our blades cut through the design of a previous digger,
rotting boards, rocks, earthworms big as young snakes;
a tarnished spoon, pink champagne foil from a party;
a palmful of blue feathers from a dead jay.

We dug and planted; we intend to have a history here
behind this rented house. Despite the owner there is a secret
between us and the ground. In the wet dirt, our fleshy bulbs
and the pink cloves of garlic are making nests of roots.

The fact of the garden has satisfied me all morning:
that we worked side by side, your name round
when I spoke it; that my fingers worked in the dirt like rain,
the ground like a made bed with its mulch of leaves,
orderly, full of possibilities, acts of love
not yet performed.

Now the water splat
on my window has made me think of something else, suddenly,
what I don't want to, the way I wake up in the night,
think I've heard a gun shot.
The memory of the news story
you told me, a week ago: the farmers south,
far south, El Salvador, afraid to go into their fields.
What does their dirt look like? I don't know.
Instead I see that some thing is being planted:
U.S. soldiers watching as others bury a dead
hand, arm, head, torso.

To be afraid
to put your hand into the dirt. To be afraid to go
look at your ground: that it has been cut like skin,
will bulge out like cut muscle: that on a fair day
there will be subterranean thunder, then a loud, continuous
hiss of blood.
I wish I could think only of the flowering
bulbs voluptuous in the spring.

The government has dug
into the lawn at the White House, planted ground-to-air
missiles, stony heads, near the beds of ceremonial tulips.

At any jet rumble I look for their armless bodies
rising to kill.
What is planted is what comes.
In the fall plant stones; in the winter the ground gapes
with stones like teeth.
They are fortifying public buildings
against people who would make history different:
concrete barricades as if we were trucks thundering dynamite.

I hold to the plan we thought of: small: full
of possibilities against despair:
us handing out
sheets of paper, thousands: the list of crimes:
sharp thin papers delving up something in people
in parking lots, shopping malls.
What will come of this?
perhaps people to stand with us outside the buildings,
to say again: *Not in my name*: words adamant
as rock. And that, here, in the coldest months,
before soldiers move again in the fields to the south.

12/14/1983

NEW YEAR'S, 1984

I avoid the stalled elevator, walk up five flights,
down a long green hall smelling of cooked food
(not cabbage) to have, in my apartment, a night view of
monuments, and public buildings with windows gunslitted
like forts.
                    Even though officially War Is Peace,
MX missiles and Marines with guns are Peacekeepers,
and the enemy is a devil with a name not like ours;

even when occasionally a helicopter spotlight
chops through my window, silver-white cuts across
my hands at the typewriter, the nightmare of caught
at the truth, naked as with a lover;
                                        even when
a trapped voice shouts on the other side of my bedroom wall:
They control us like robots;
                                        I do not agree
with my neighbor, I do not agree with my government.

I agree with you, mother-naked on the year's first night.
I agree with your hand in my cunt. Your fingers explain
the future by scrawling lines of exquisite pleasure
on the walls of my vagina, urgent graffiti.
                                        The day
that comes, as it will, when a neighbor or a casual laughing
hating mouth offers to let me pass, if I say *Her
not me*, if I agree to rat-tooth jaws closing
on you as enemy, Jew, dyke:
                                        then I will remember
your hand has written your name inside me forever.

1/9/84

ON SUGAR LOAF KEY

You are snoring mildly in the bed where we devoured
each other two years ago. One red hibiscus
gaped then at our love and ignorance.
How well do we know each other now?

We play at questions like the TV host asks the nervous
couple: *Would you know me in the dark in a strange tent?*
Could you find me in a hundred thousand at a demonstration?

Jane knew Barbara across the width of a mob's curses
by the back of her head. I would know your hip motion,
your alternate strong haunches walking, and at night.

If I came back to bed in the leaf-sifted light,
the air ripe with night's water and the sun,

if I lay close with closed eyes, I would know you by smell:
the roused dirt, the earliest water, my face near the earliest smell.

2/14/1984

KINKY SEX

When I'm gone from you my hair
will keep growing, like seeds
in the garden, my slinky head hair
three kinds of morning glory,
my armpit hairs waggling
as they sprout.
By the time you see
the tufts of my toes again,
they'll have jumped in Gulf water
and my lanky leg hairs in the Atlantic.
My nose hairs will have twitched
in salt air.
By the time I come home,
forearms lush as a vacationer's lawn,
cunt hairs curled and kinky,
the ivy in the backyard will envy me.

When I get back, water me with kisses
and you can choose whichever you want,
eyebrows to crunch like tiny dill seeds,
or my bristly asshole hairs, thistly,
or a breast hair, wispy grass stalk
to pull between your teeth.

5/30/1984

BEFORE ME

Elana's album opens to your photograph
under cellophane. You are suntanned,
younger. I am jealous of your smile
diagonal toward someone just outside
the frame, maybe the lover before me.
It was that year, the trip through Oregon.

I am jealous of any moment in your life
that I haven't been in. I want to steal
the photograph and pretend
you were smiling at the thought of me.

6/9/1984

WHAT I REMEMBER

In the middle of the fight you left me
and came back with your camera.

My face was runny with tears, saliva,
and stubborn with grief. I put my hands
over my eyes, so you couldn't see me.

In your hands the camera clicked
like a clock about to strike the hour,
a picture of one moment in the long circle
of time together.
                              You shifted to my side
of the bed, closer in the spilled light,
and said: *This means we'll get through it.*

I was not convinced. What had you seen
when you looked at me through your lens?

Now I don't remember why I was crying.
By now you've probably unwound
the dripping film and hung it to dry
in the darkroom. I imagine you looking
for my face in the slippery sequence of moments.

6/9/1984

FRIDAY NIGHT

The sun is going down red-hot, swollen
with what chances for the day didn't get taken,
lottery tickets that didn't get bought.

I wonder if the moon will push up full
in the west like a weightlifter,
a pregnant lady, at what time tonight.

Maybe you'll see her in San Francisco
at your birthday supper and she'll watch
you unwind snails from their clocks of shells.

Forty years ago maybe she was a cold magnet
that pulled you out of your mother and left,
showed you the back of her head,

then her face once a month. Tonight
she's looking for you. She can see through white
walls and cabinet doors, where pictures you've made

wait for you to choose which will stretch
like a small moon out of the swimming darkness,
develop the muscles of lights and shadows.

But the moon is looking for you. In all the shadows
in this town she misses the one happenstance
she wishes to see, what she has made:

you, how handsome, herself in an earth mirror.
She wants to boast about you to herself.
She's got her eye out for you tonight.

7/13/1984

DONE

When you're gone out of town, the way I get you back is
I masturbate. If you're away this week, next week, no matter.
I raise one hand. In a second it's your tongue on my clitoris,
your head's weight on my lap in the striped pink armchair,
your jaw opening like a thought between my thighs, lower,
your tongue a delicate knifeblade licking stone. My wetness
eases your work. My blood satisfies the heat with a tremor.
You lift your head. Done, my hands lift.
Under my ass there is a cold damp like saliva. Nothing else left.

Back, at 2 a.m., you're more than the sharp memory I angled
between my legs, sensation after the day's numb headlines.
Your hand sweats and dreams on my stomach, not your imagined
hand in my jeans in the backyard dark, no clandestine
act while above us a neighbor's cigarette shines red.
In the garden a moonflower is stretching its jaws in the cold,
its smell of my mother's face powder, its skin like your skin.
I drowse. Everything outside this room is alone.
I move. You say my name. Your hip backs me like warm stone.

10/7/1984

NOT THE END OF THE STORY

Lying on you naked, naked skin to skin,
as on damp ground in early evening, or at the bottom of a well
that seeps cool water sweat at summer's dry end.
The candle burns down low, a blue methyl beryl
flame deep in the well. In the story the witch said
dig up my garden, split my wood, go fetch
my blue light that never goes out, lost in the well.

Deep under me, you breathe out words to catch
my hands. The night fills up with rain, a soft risk
against the brick walls of sky. You sleep. The flame
is shaking blue, my last pleasure of the night: to watch
with my face sideways on your breast, your skin calm
as wet dirt under me, to go to sleep before the candle goes out.

10/28/1984

BY THE CORNER AT F STREET

By the corner at F Street the unseasonable wind jostles
branches on the hawtree, unleafed almost bare in the sun,
like your shirtsleeve rolled-up forearms, hot weather arms.

I'd fit my palm in the secret vee of your elbow
for the sweat of your skin, if you were walking with me.
Inside the alley I shiver. The wind drops its pretense of summer.

Someone has boarded up the dark cave triangle opening
in the corner wall: no bums, no summer unventilated heat
prostration, no small fire or amputated feet this winter,

no reeking bottles smashed on the smashed bricks.
The wind flaps a loose board in the plywood patchwork
showing someone's cold hand and arm and unhomed body

a way out of the wind. T.C. wouldn't say where he slept
but he was pleased to shake hands after our conversation.
The yellow plastic clinic bracelet trembled on his wrist.

In my rooms, the radiator sizzles like a hot skillet. Heat
comes with the rent: how I afford a place for shedding winter
down to the glamour of your naked shoulders in the kitchen.

I have enough covers to warm up one stark wall
with the red crazy patchwork quilt. Easy to wait for you
inside, drinking hot tea behind my thick door.

Across from the movies at the Circle a raft of women
sleep in the lit shelter of a doorway. Tonight
we won't see their bundles puff in the wind like sails.

At the polling place we ask for votes for the woman
who believes in bottle deposits: so people on the street

can pick up a little money. The wind says something

louder than I can hear. Some well-dressed white voters shrink
their coats away: in our boots and knit caps we look
like we've never sat behind a coffee table. Some look past us,

as I did the woman heaped like a bag of her clothes
on the bench, November, only her eye animate and bare.
In the streetlight dark, I can scarcely see your eyes,

as you shout some encouragement over the bitter wind.

12/4/1984

IN THE MORNING, THE ROOM SHIFTS

In your photographs of other lovers, I can see the desire.
And in those not of your lovers? Nevertheless, there
it is: the sexual desire, as distinct as light suspended
in the milky silver colloids of exposed film: the moment's
aura of desire when you make a picture.
                                                                    In this one, inside
the photographic white border, inside the mirror's wooden frame
where we sit naked, I am blessed by more than the excessive bright
morning sun's corona along my back and hip. Over our heads
hovers an image painted into the mirror's mercurial haze:
a small wicker basket full of grapes and peaches and a mess
of vines.
            With your camera, you are arm angled at the instant:
focus, and shutter close, us at the pattern's center, incandescent
mandala of our twined legs, my just caressed pouching stomach,
our perfected breasts.
                                        I am watching myself and you summon
a moment that goes on and on, like the chimed brass
we ring at morning meditation. I listen as the sound extends
beyond my best hearing.
                                             And I swallow it: yes,
with greed, with sexual desire. The image sits in my stomach,
not a pregnant low bulging, but under my breastbone. It expands
like other moments grown to poems: me holding a peach, plumped
in my hand like a heart: or my friend, a girl fetal with shame
on the floor of an attic closet. Images like the dangerous
warned-against seeds of childhood that sprout in the guts.

And this image: desire: a gesture at the moment's edge,
like the fox-grape vine prying in under the window-frame,
like my hand pushing the wooden shutter open, past the window ledge.

1/17/1985

READING MAPS: THREE

for Joan

By the map, Point Lookout is almost an island in the bay,
land clenched between two river thighs, Patuxent, Potomac.

The road runs into what looks like ocean by its heave,
pause, and collapse. Rain spatters on the car roof,
an echo of radio clatter an hour ago: gunfire, machine
guns, U.S. soldiers landing in Grenada.
                                        To a woman
not here, known to me only from a distance, I say: *I'm sorry,*
I'm sorry:
            and lean into thousand-miled grey water,
blank as unfocused TV screen. What is happening there?
on her mother's island, the small place marked by her words
in the map of her stories: what inside the coral reef surf
or by the limetrees where dark women pause in sharp sun,
work in their hands, the children of their hands nearby,
as the assault begins, blades of air slung from helicopters.

Here a salty wind thrashes and whistles, no bullets.
Behind me gulls hang and creak in the wind like old doors
shutting. A door slams behind me:
                                    home, after school,
getting to be a grown girl, I iron the cotton sheets
into perfect blankness. No thump shakes Laura, dreaming
in the straight-backed chair, upright, eyes closed, dark-brown
face crumpled in an hour's rest from generations of children.

I look at her sideways, the woman hired to raise me.
She knew me before I knew myself. Which lines am I
in her face? I can't look her in the face: the mystery
of her living.
              Now I can only guess at what memory opened
in her sleep. Perhaps she heard another door close:

a muffled thump. The oldest girl hides with the children, tumbled
shadows in the dirty clothes under the bed, rustbrown
caught in the broken springs. The white man's patched
boot squeaks by, her mother's pleading ends, broken.
By spring the farm is taken; they leave the sloping porch
and go.
Not her story: another woman, year, South
Carolina, not Mississippi. Laura never told me. I am guessing
because today, on the island far south, there is the slam:

the foot, boot, kicks down a fragile door.

I saw her,
last, tied to a chair, kept from wandering where she pleased:
down the anonymous nursing home hall, an old woman
in a knit cap, struggle with hidden straps, an orange bedspread
in her room, chenille, no pictures, no photographs on the wall.
Her eyes, blank, then briefly sharp as thorns, catch me;
her hands grip mine: woody old vines, vital, knotty,
bind me in the swamp: my terror that I can no longer deny
I am a child of hers.
The world says it is not so,
but she says: *So bad, so bad. So good, so good. Mama,
mama, mama.* Her mouth fumbles. Is it her, her mother,
my mother, her children, me?
But I know who I am,
even as I pry her winding tenacious fingers from my hand.

I am the one, flat on my back, the faces of dark women
leaning over, three women in green smocks, on duty, unknown,
as I lie mired in my own shit, urine, blood, salty pain.
With tender words they are not paid to utter, they instruct
how to shape and expel the secret: *Bear down, baby, bear
down, bear down.* Their hands grip both my hands:
no straps on my wrists, they guide me through chaos,
quagmire and thicket of my flesh. I crack and sink.
Their eyes far above, steady as birds in a shaking treetop,
continue to know and save me.
Done, delivered, I am
severed and forget them: servants in the night labor room.
Perhaps, off duty at dawn, they wash their hands of me:
an ignorant white yelling girl.

I'm sorry it's happening
again, I say to the wind, breath of my betrayed mothers.

They are elsewhere, shaping words, or clay into new pots,
or steadying spirits in the dissolved clay of old bodies;
they pick up plates shattered when the door broke, pick
themselves up from the cleanswept dirt floor:
while I stand
asking from their hands.
I am of their hands. I must do
with my own, out from this almost-island of sorrow.

The waves sketch
lines on the narrow sand, a map of foam given and taken
by the water, pattern of nowhere to go.
I drive the way out:
black asphalt road, past a stand of pines, windbent green
sails on land at tenuous anchor.
The rosin-tarred trunks
mark graves of men from another century's war, prisoners
who carved chessmen, or, in letters home to Alabama, craved
butter, red peppers, sage, onions, honey, sweet potatoes.

As they lay, midnight, no blanket but salt spray, the wind
whistling off the water to pin them to the ground; or lay,
daylight, dying, vomit, white skin putrid with small pox;
did any feel the land swell under him, the sea journey,
midnight in the hold, dark skin rotted in excrement, land-
fall to live as captive beast? Did any confess the secret,
the fear he died for, rather than say he was wrong?

No words
here, nothing carved on a pine trunk marker, nothing
except deaths named on a pale shaft of granite.
No grave
open like the ones being dug in Grenada, ready to speak,
split wombs of earth; no grave like that of my father,
him just closed with his secrets inside a mouth of red clay.

My blood his, my heart a small coffin-box given by him,
his voice muffled between my breasts. Is he saying *Mama*?
Is he crying *I'm sorry*? Does he mutter stories of bestial acts,

the white woman vanished into the swamp, black alligator-
men, and her white nape all bloody? Is he turning, restless,
under the look of men who shovel red dirt on the grave,
servant eyes that know more than him, black crow eyes
that see down to the bone?
                                        I don't know what he knew
at the end. Years ago his voice was staccato as radio
propaganda: *We are waging a war against beasts of prey.*

In Grenada, young men, white as parachute sails, float
to the ground, and point cold steel-blue fear, and fire
at brown, black, yellow, red: commies, animals.
They say: *Our land, our women. Our job is to kill
people and destroy things. We will bury you.*

Where can I lay down the weight of this sorrow? I've travelled
south, miles, looking, on bridges suspended like riddles
between green islands, through red mangrove, black mangrove,
root snakes on either side. I've dreamed of islands deep
in the great swamp's belly, safety where the land trembles
and earth fragments break free.
                                                    Some delicately balance,
matted with yellow lilies: by day, small floating countries;
by night, sinking in clouds of blue flame, will-o-the-wisps.

Others bloom and rot and grow substantial, clumps of maple,
tall leafy wings that catch the wind: these islands journey.
I could track one at night by rank sweet musk smell.
I could not be followed. By day and night, the patterns
of water and dirt alter; the tangled passages snare
all memory.
                    I would choose an island for me and my lover,
and lay myself down there, lightly, light-hearted, naked
in the place of no more crying, in warm burrows of grass,
coarse thickets, blankets. We would eat blackberries,
speckled marsh eggs, hoecake while the cornmeal lasted.
In the winter, a fringe of green in the ice, the inexplicable
pucker of water from an unknown source, a trickle of river
beginning, and our desire. And if terror in desire, ours,
not another's.

The alligator nothing but itself
sunk deep, the silver coin of its eye shining in the mud,
its silent drift up like a log, its metal-trap teeth
snap at a heron's reedy leg, its soft grunt like a pig.

Ourselves, sheltered in dry grass, grunting a little
in sex, four breasts tumbling. No one's boot to poke us
and him say *animals*.
Toward sunset, shrill voices
from far away would come closer: shrieking, praying, whistling,
clicking, blackbirds and grackles, to knit and ravel patterns
in the air: women, escaped from locked-up or hiding,
and flying to roost. Now they fall from the sky, flash
of wings, hair, arms, into the rustling trees, all resting,
no door to lock, night in the swamp.
We two would watch,
gathered safe, blue night pulled over us like a worn spread.

A dream, a place I've never come to, though I've travelled
miles. I've gone to the very end of land in the night,
one road only behind and before me, no guidance from the stars
staring down through ragged clouds, a million drifting
eyes looking up from the water.
I've come to the coral island
where a woman lived, old enough to be my mother, but not mine,
Barbara. At night I went to her door to ask for the secret:
how to find a place without sorrow.
In the morning humid light
I saw in the yard the little papaya with green breasts dangling;
in the house, a cluttered table, a pink hibiscus mouth,
a cracked cup still in use, books, a creased yellow
map of the island. I sat at the table ready for truth,
for directions. In her quavery voice, she told a story:

that once there was a man who wanted to live forever,
so he wrapped his heart up in a cloth, locked it in a box,
box slid into a chest, chest pushed into a closet,
door closed and locked. He lived on, his heart safe
(he thought) as a vireo whistling in a gumbo limbo tree
on an island in swamp water. But he couldn't hear his heart
beating, and forgot where he'd put it. He forgot to look.

His secret heart shrivelled to a lump of dried red clay,
and he died.
                    Later she told: of years her muscles clenched,
tight ropes of flesh, guarding her secret's escape:
her daytime fear of stares like thrown rocks, the bolted
door, the dreams of surveillance at night, searchlights pushing
at the window, malignant faces as she touched her lover, hand
resting on the hip of the woman by her, curved earth horizon.

She cast the secret of her love, finally, into a pool of silence,
a listening circle of women. Released, dizzy, her body
flew open. She unlocked herself in a new place with the others.

Of the way there, she replied: *Tell me your piece of the truth.*

Today, now, no answer. The radio chatters gunfire.
Waves open and shut meaningless noisy mouths on the sand.
From the end of land, I drive the question, road curved
toward home, north, past the bony shaking pines, past
the sandy fields, tobacco sheds, irrigation ponds,

past the swamps of the Patuxent: the place of the Piscataway
and the Nanticoke, of fugitives, and runaway slaves: their homes
built in the low places: corn patches, pigs, rockfish
in hand's reach, the children raised under no owner,
maple seeds into wings like green grasshoppers, summer
fevers, the messages, plans for rebellion and freeing the land,
the sudden bloody raids by armed white men, capture
or escape;
                    by fall, the brief grass shelters overrun
with catbrier, bullbrier, wild grape, and the struggle begun
somewhere else, a river lowland, the Mobile, the Tombigbee,
or in the river of grass, Pahokee, Okeefenokee, or north
along the Savannah, the Altamaha, the Cape Fear, the Mattaponi,
the Potomac.

                    I drive north toward that old swamp, the city
with monuments squatting huge as gravestones, its central dome
built with slave labor.
                              I imagine green snakey
kudzu vines wrapping the marble office buildings,

sarcophagi: no one in or out, no devouring
war, no mechanical heart beat of helicopters thudding
over the beaches of a small green island no wider than the city.

This afternoon, the numbness of repetition: despisal, attack,
theft of another's life, the boast of violence happening
again.
        But I have a few images I keep against despair,
sharp as glass shattered on city streets, bits glittering
like mica in the squared cracks of pavement, and pieces embedded
in the clay path through a vacant lot, unfinished mosaics,
stories of those walking between the streets, feet that wear
the glass fragments smooth as the river;
                                        a block from my house,
the women's shelter, wire mesh on the windows against men,
steel mesh fence, but the wash hung out, the white, plaid, checkered wash
flapping, unwearied as clouds;
                                under a glass roof,
my mother and I together, leaning wordless over the orchids,
lemon, orange, white, purple-throated, the close fragrant
domed damp, the mosses, a trickle of water in the greenhouse;

on the river, my oldest child rowing, water-strider
under cement and iron bridges, his wooden blades' stroke
through reflected surface, his care with the water, its currents,
his balance, eye on me; and his brother keeping me
company on the jumbled rocks, our talk, poke at the trash,
the flat black rocks we skim like tiny birds on the water;

by the river, trembling earth under our feet, my lover and me
at what used to be a dump, rusty cans, sludge turned back
to marsh, refuge, islands, pools where lily leaves stick up
pink veined ears, and frogs out of the bottom mud squeak
directions, *wichity-wichity*, near where we sit down
on a small cloth of dry grass, holding hands, risky
under the stares of those walking by;

                                    and long ago,
with my girlfriend, us not quite grown, in the abandoned house,
graffiti, forbidden red and black on the wall, the cold,
the rotten linoleum, us shivering as we cleared a space to sit

in the empty room full of what could happen;
                                        in two years,
her flight, runaway from the small town, assembly line,
rest of life in the factory squaring children's blocks,
or in a house crammed with children: the police found her crouched,
fetal behind an attic door, no money, no place to go:

I didn't ask her what had happened. *I give up on her*
were the words I wrote in my notebook. We were alike, too close;
she might drag me down. I had plans for myself, I had the means
to make my escape.
                    Twenty years later, she called; she said:
I gave up on you.
                    The spring when I was out, walking,
and saw him open the car door for you; you got in;
he closed the door; and you drove off with him. That was when
I gave up on you.
                    Later she spoke of a woman on the ward
who'd come in with razor-marked skin, her sketch of her life's
bloody map.
            She asked: *What will happen different, now*?

Later we talked of how we had danced, two girls,
the galloping, staggering wheel of a polka, our thighs clearing
a wider and wider space on the cold slippery floor.

1985

Other titles from Firebrand Books include:

Artemis In Echo Park, Poetry by Eloise Klein Healy/$8.95
Beneath My Heart, Poetry by Janice Gould/$8.95
The Big Mama Stories by Shay Youngblood/$8.95
A Burst Of Light, Essays by Audre Lorde/$7.95
Cecile, Stories by Ruthann Robson/$8.95
Crime Against Nature, Poetry by Minnie Bruce Pratt/$8.95
Diamonds Are A Dyke's Best Friend by Yvonne Zipter/$9.95
Dykes To Watch Out For, Cartoons by Alison Bechdel/$6.95
Dykes To Watch Out For: The Sequel, Cartoons by Alison Bechdel/$8.95
Exile In The Promised Land, A Memoir by Marcia Freedman/$8.95
Eye Of A Hurricane, Stories by Ruthann Robson/$8.95
The Fires Of Bride, A Novel by Ellen Galford/$8.95
Food & Spirits, Stories by Beth Brant *(Degonwadonti)*/$8.95
Free Ride, A Novel by Marilyn Gayle/$9.95
A Gathering Of Spirit, A Collection by North American Indian Women edited by Beth Brant *(Degonwadonti)*/$10.95
Getting Home Alive by Aurora Levins Morales and Rosario Morales/$9.95
The Gilda Stories, A Novel by Jewelle Gomez/$9.95
Good Enough To Eat, A Novel by Lesléa Newman/$8.95
Humid Pitch, Narrative Poetry by Cheryl Clarke/$8.95
Jewish Women's Call For Peace edited by Rita Falbel, Irena Klepfisz, and Donna Nevel/$4.95
Jonestown & Other Madness, Poetry by Pat Parker/$7.95
Just Say Yes, A Novel by Judith McDaniel/$8.95
The Land Of Look Behind, Prose and Poetry by Michelle Cliff/$8.95
Legal Tender, A Mystery by Marion Foster/$9.95
Lesbian (Out)law, Survival Under the Rule of Law by Ruthann Robson/$9.95
A Letter To Harvey Milk, Short Stories by Lesléa Newman/$8.95
Letting In The Night, A Novel by Joan Lindau/$8.95
Living As A Lesbian, Poetry by Cheryl Clarke/$7.95
Making It, A Woman's Guide to Sex in the Age of AIDS by Cindy Patton and Janis Kelly/$4.95
Metamorphosis, Reflections On Recovery by Judith McDaniel/$7.95
Mohawk Trail by Beth Brant *(Degonwadonti)*/$7.95
Moll Cutpurse, A Novel by Ellen Galford/$7.95
The Monarchs Are Flying, A Novel by Marion Foster/$8.95
More Dykes To Watch Out For, Cartoons by Alison Bechdel/$7.95
Movement In Black, Poetry by Pat Parker/$8.95
My Mama's Dead Squirrel, Lesbian Essays on Southern Culture by Mab Segrest /$9.95